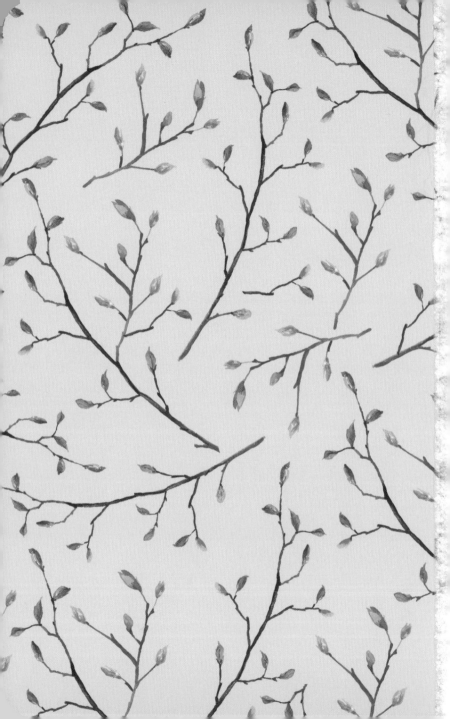

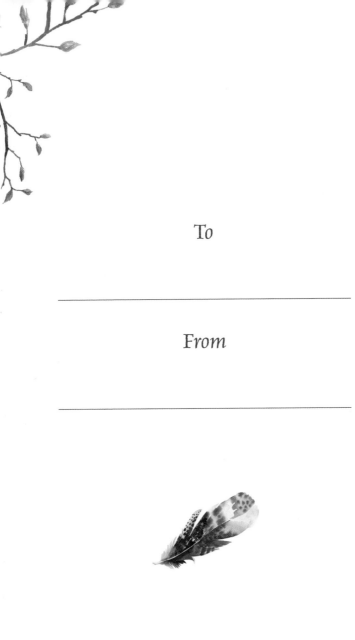

To

_____

From

_____

Everyday Grace

60 DEVOTIONS

Ellie Claire® Gift & Paper Expressions
Franklin, TN 37067
EllieClaire.com
Ellie Claire is a registered trademark of Worthy Media, Inc.

Everyday Grace
© 2016 by Ellie Claire
Published by Ellie Claire, an imprint of Worthy Publishing Group,
a division of Worthy Media, Inc.

ISBN 978-1-63326-125-9

Excluding Scripture verses and deity pronouns, in some quotations references to men and masculine pronouns have been replaced with gender-neutral or feminine references. Additionally, in some quotations we have carefully updated verb forms and wording that may distract modern readers.

Stock or custom editions of Ellie Claire titles may be purchased in bulk for educational, business, ministry, fundraising, or sales promotional use. For information, please e-mail info@EllieClaire.com

Cover and interior art by Shutterstock | shutterstock.com

Typesetting by Jeff Jansen | AestheticSoup.net

Compiled by Jill Olson

Printed in China

5 6 7 8 9 – 21 20 19 18

*L*ike any other gift, the gift of grace
can be yours only if you'll reach out
and take it. Maybe being able to
reach out and take it is a gift too.

FREDERICK BUECHNER

That Type of Father

You have also given me the shield of Your salvation, and Your right hand upholds me; and Your gentleness makes me great.

PSALM 18:35 NASB

God is both patient and kind. He's not a quick-tempered parent, expecting you to do things perfectly. He's the one holding your hand as you learn to walk. Helping you move forward one step at a time. Picking you up when you fall. Cheering you on when you get discouraged. Whispering, "You can do it!" when you need to hear it most.

God knows what you're capable of, for better or worse. Though He desires great things from you, He knows the learning curve of life can be steep. He's fully aware of your fears, your failures, your weaknesses, and even your secrets. He doesn't hold them against you. He fully loves and accepts you. That's why He wants to help you get rid of anything that's preventing you from holding on tightly to Him.

God's patient love is a safety net that allows you to risk living the life He's planned for you. Just keep walking, and hold on tight.

Dear heavenly Father, help me hold on to You and let go of…

Don't we all long for a father...who cares for us in spite of our failures? We do have that type of a father. A father who is at His best when we are at our worst...whose grace is strongest when our devotion is weakest.

MAX LUCADO

We have missed the full impact of the Gospel if we have not discovered what it is to be ourselves, loved by God, irreplaceable in His sight, unique among our fellow humans.

BRUCE LARSON

Incredible as it may seem, God wants our companionship. He wants to have us close to Him. He wants to be a father to us, to shield us, to protect us, to counsel us, and to guide us in our way through life.

BILLY GRAHAM

His Way of Working

Anyone who belongs to Christ has become a new person.
The old life is gone; a new life has begun!

2 CORINTHIANS 5:17 NLT

Whether your responsibilities lie inside or outside the home (or both!), you probably have a preferred way of working. You might like to work alone, or in a group; according to plan, or by intuition; under guidelines, or without constraint.

Your heavenly Father, too, has a preferred way of working. While He sometimes intervenes dramatically in a person's life, most of the time He chooses to advance slowly, gently, and modestly into the hearts and minds of His loved ones. Day by day, His Spirit moves to clear confusion, lift regret, dry tears, and provide hope to the awakening soul. There's little fanfare when God works in His usual way, but there's subtle, significant, and long-lasting change taking place.

You may not notice all the spiritual growth taking place in you every day, but it's happening as you think more deeply about God and His presence in your life. It continues as you respond to His work by reaching out to others with kindness, thoughtfulness, and love.

Dear Lord, I have discovered You at work in…

As our love for the Lord increases and our knowledge
of His Word deepens, we have more to offer
the body of Christ…. That's why Paul
urges us to press on, show up, keep going.

LIZ CURTIS HIGGS

So faith bounds forward to its goal in God,
and love can trust the Lord to lead her there;
upheld by Him my soul is following hard,
till God has fully fulfilled my deepest prayer.

FREDERICK BROOK

There is no unbelief.
Whoever plants a seed beneath the sod,
And waits to see it push away the clod,
He trusts in God.

ELIZABETH YORK CASE

All of You

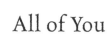

Each time he said, "My grace is all you need.
My power works best in weakness."

2 CORINTHIANS 12:9 NLT

Porcelain is known for its strength and translucence. Of course, strength is a relative term. While porcelain is strong for fired clay, it easily chips, cracks, and breaks. It will never win a battle against a slate floor. But this weakness doesn't make porcelain less attractive or desirable. In fact, its delicacy adds to its beauty. Fine porcelain is so translucent that the shadow of the hand of the one holding it can be seen right through it.

The same can be said of you. It's true that God's a source of strength. But you're still fragile. Even your areas of greatest strength hold weaknesses and vulnerabilities. But God can use all of who you are, even your weaknesses, to do amazing things.

When you feel small or incapable of handling a task you know you have to face, pray for God's power to work mightily in your life. But remember to look for the shadow of His hand, gently holding you close. When you're weak, God's strength has a chance to shine through you in unexpectedly beautiful ways.

God, the weakness it's hardest to trust You with is…

Each one of us is God's special work of art.
Through us, He teaches and inspires, delights
and encourages, informs and uplifts all those who view
our lives. God, the master artist, is most concerned about
expressing Himself—His thoughts and His intentions—
through what He paints in our character.... [He] wants
to paint a beautiful portrait of His Son in and through
your life. A painting like no other in all of time.

JONI EARECKSON TADA

It is not what we do that matters,
but what a sovereign God chooses to do through us.
God doesn't want our success; He wants us.

CHARLES COLSON

11

In the Details

*Many, O Lord my God, are the wonders which
You have done, and Your thoughts toward us;
there is none to compare with You. If I would declare
and speak of them, they would be too numerous to count.*

PSALM 40:5 NASB

If you want to do things exactly right, you know you need to pay attention to detail. A workable budget takes accurate numbers and a successful recipe calls for precise measurements, as does a prize-winning quilt or well-fitted garment. Without seeing to the details, the big picture won't come out as intended.

In the big picture of your life, details also matter. That's why God invites you to bring not only the heavy burdens of your heart to Him, but those small, niggling fears too. He opens His ears to whatever bothers you, from minor annoyances to major irritants. If it's important enough to occupy your thoughts, it's important enough to engage you in prayer.

The details of the lives of others are important to God, too, and He may use you to respond in precise and specific ways. One example: a friend's illness prompts you to bring her a meal. Another: a loved one's disappointment leads you to spend extra time with her. Small details? No, not to the ones you serve nor to God.

The small thing, Lord, that is bothering me today is…

Prayer enlarges the heart until it is capable
of containing God's gift of Himself. Ask and seek,
and your heart will grow big enough to receive Him
and keep Him as your own.

MOTHER TERESA

By Jesus's gracious, kindly Spirit, He moves in our lives
sharing His very own life with us.... He introduces
the exotic fruits of His own person into the prepared soil
of our hearts; there they take root and flourish.

W. PHILIP KELLER

God of Help

My help comes from the Lord, *who made heaven and earth.*

PSALM 121:2 ESV

By now, no doubt you have come to realize that your God is a helpful God. Rather than sitting high in heaven and watching you struggle to follow Him, He gets right down where you are and clears the way ahead of you.

God's Son Jesus walked among people to prove the reality of God's presence here on earth. Jesus demonstrated God's concern for everyday women and men by healing, restoring, and renewing broken lives. He welcomed children and covered them with His blessing. Wherever He went, Jesus helped others discover and draw closer to His caring, compassionate Father.

Through His Holy Spirit, God stands ready to help you deepen your understanding of Him and His work in your life. Wherever you are, whatever challenges you face, and however many tears have fallen from your eyes, God is there to help you with His comfort and strength.

Open your arms to His help—and then keep them open for someone else. It's the way people come to know the reality of our very helpful God.

Today, Lord, please help me with...

In difficulties, I can drink freely of God's power
and experience His touch of refreshment and blessing—
much like an invigorating early spring rain.

ANABEL GILLHAM

God is a rich and bountiful Father, and He does not
forget His children, nor withhold from them anything
which it would be to their advantage to receive.

J. K. MACLEAN

Be assured, if you walk with Him and look to Him
and expect help from Him, He will never fail you.

GEORGE MUELLER

God is the God of promise. He keeps His word,
even when that seems impossible.

COLIN URQUHART

God of Hope

You have seen me tossing and turning through the night.
You have collected all my tears and preserved them in your bottle!
You have recorded every one in your book.

PSALM 56:8 TLB

It might be said that the only true remedy for any disaster is hope. Without hope, a devastated landmark would remain in ruins forever, and a broken heart would never recover. Hope enables us to envision a better future, hope propels us forward, and hope motivates us to turn our dreams into reality.

God offers an even more remarkable hope. In the heart of the child who has endured much, His hope enables her to imagine better and to take her place among survivors and achievers. In the heart of the adult who has been cast off and left alone, His hope enables her to believe in herself and walk with grace and dignity. His hope is for anyone who has known what it's like to cry, because His hope dries tears and comforts the downcast spirit.

In the world, as in your life, God has not promised to solve every problem, settle every conflict, or alleviate every injustice. But He does give this to you in abundance—life-giving, life-saving hope.

Lord God, I want to bring Your hope to...

Let your faith in Christ...be in the quiet confidence
that He will every day and every moment keep you
as the apple of His eye, keep you in perfect peace
and in the sure experience of all the light
and the strength you need in His service.

ANDREW MURRAY

God Incarnate is the end of fear; and the heart
that realizes that He is in the midst, that takes heed
to the assurance of His loving presence,
will be quiet in the midst of alarm.

F. B. MEYER

Do not be afraid to enter the cloud that
is settling down on your life. God is in it.
The other side is radiant with His glory.

L. B. COWMAN

Grace comes free of charge
to people who do not
deserve it, and I am one
of those people....

PHILIP YANCEY

Sound in the Silence

The Spirit himself intercedes for us
with groanings too deep for words.

ROMANS 8:26 ESV

At times of extraordinary joy or surprise, shock or sorrow, emotions are difficult to express. We just can't seem to find the right words to say how we feel.

Similarly, there may be times when you find it impossible to pray because you don't know what to say. You yearn to reveal your inmost thoughts to God, but the words that come to mind fall short of your true feelings and fail to get to the bottom of your anguish.

When you step into God's presence in prayer, think of yourself as sitting with a friend who has known you from before you can remember (He has), and who understands your deepest feelings and tears (He does). Silence is comfortable when you're with this kind of friend, and silence is comfortable with God. He can hear unspoken words, and He will respond to you in ways far beyond words.

A heart, buoyant with inexpressible joy or even burdened with indefinable sadness, is all you need to bring to Him. He will know exactly what you mean.

Lord, if I sit in silence with You this week it is because…

God desires that every servant of His would understand and perform this blessed practice, that His church would know how to train its children to recognize this high and holy privilege, and that every believer would realize the importance of making time for God alone.

L. B. COWMAN

A living, loving God can and does make His presence felt, can and does speak to us in the silence of our hearts, can and does warm and caress us till we no longer doubt that He is near, that He is here.

BRENNAN MANNING

God listens in compassion and love, just like we do when our children come to us. He delights in our presence.

RICHARD J. FOSTER

Plan of Escape

The Lord knows how to deliver the godly out of temptations.

2 PETER 2:9 NKJV

Most of us have taken emergency workers' advice and thought about how we would get out of our home in case of fire. Though a house fire may never occur, we are wise to have an escape plan in place for our family and ourselves.

Spiritually, God has put an escape plan in place for you in case of temptation of any kind. His plan shows you the quickest way out of guilt and confusion and into the safety and security of His loving presence.

His plan is this: When tempted, leave immediately, whether from a physical place or an emotional state of mind, and run (not walk) to your heavenly Father's arms. Take whatever troubles you have to Him in prayer and then stay where you are until the way forward is clear. He may choose to soothe you with an outpouring of His Spirit, or with the strengthening words of Scripture, or with the counsel of a wise and spiritually mature friend.

Before you face temptation, know your plan of escape—He'll be there for you.

Dear God, I feel in spiritual danger when…

God is waiting for us to come to Him with our needs....
God's throne room is always open.... Every single believer
in the whole world could walk into the throne room
all at one time, and it would not even be crowded.

CHARLES STANLEY

Our faithfulness to Christ is clearly
and unmistakably demonstrated by the degree
to which we have accepted and granted forgiveness.

STEPHEN ARTERBURN

There are no "ifs" in God's Kingdom.
His timing is perfect. His will is our hiding place.
Lord Jesus, keep me in Your will! Don't let me
go mad by poking about outside it.

CORRIE TEN BOOM

The Ripple Effect

*Dear brothers and sisters, pattern your lives after mine,
and learn from those who follow our example.*

PHILIPPIANS 3:17 NLT

As you recognize more clearly the beauty of the Lord and His love for you, His Spirit moves you to imitate His characteristics. His compassion for you inspires you to show more compassion to others, and His mercy toward your weaknesses enables you to deal gently with the frailties of others. Your knowledge of His presence in your life becomes the source of your genuine confidence, true security, and lasting joy.

His Spirit at work in you cannot fail to touch the lives of others. As a small pebble dropped into the middle of a pond creates ever-flowing, ever-widening ripples, the things you do make others want to imitate you—your thoughtfulness, your kindness, your gentleness, your joy in life. Their actions inspire more people, and so on!

You cannot imagine how many ripples you already have sent out among your loved ones and friends, and this side of heaven, you will never really know. But do know this: the world is a very big pond, and ripples can spread a long way out.

Praise to You, Father, because I sent out a ripple when…

Every action of our lives touches
a chord that vibrates in eternity.

EDWIN HUBBEL CHAPIN

In whatever [God] does in the course
of our lives, He gives us, through the experience,
some power to help others.

ELISABETH ELLIOT

It is through the living witness of others that we are
drawn to God at all. It is because of His creatures,
and His work in them, that we come to praise Him.

TERESA OF AVILA

25

Come In Gently

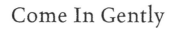

The wisdom from above is first pure,
then peaceable, gentle, open to reason,
full of mercy and good fruits, impartial and sincere.

JAMES 3:17 ESV

You might have noticed something about the Lord: He knocks, but He doesn't beat down the door if you don't answer immediately. He enters, but He doesn't sit down until you invite Him.

When the Lord steps into your life, He does so gently. He wants you to feel safe with Him and relaxed in His presence. If you're not ready to handle one of His truths or attributes yet, He takes no offense, but waits with loving patience until you want to bring up the subject. If you aren't prepared for a committed relationship right now, He won't press you, but will speak to you with inviting words and affectionate phrases. Even if you choose to ignore Him for a while, He won't bolt the door, but you'll find Him when you're ready to look for Him.

With respect for your true feelings, the Lord reveals Himself and opens the way to a relationship with Him. He knocks on the door of your heart and waits until He hears your footsteps.

Lord, come to me with gentleness and…

Herein is grace and graciousness! Herein is love
and loving kindness! How it opens to us the
compassion of Jesus—so gentle, tender, considerate!

CHARLES H. SPURGEON

I want to do what I can do to avoid having disharmony
and one of the things God has spoken to me about is voice
tones and opinions. Gentle words turn away anger
and not being overly generous with your opinion is wisdom.

JOYCE MEYER

If there are a thousand steps between us and Him,
He will take all but one. But He will leave
the final one for us. The choice is ours.

MAX LUCADO

An Uncommon Blessing

If I must boast, I will boast of the things that show my weakness.

2 CORINTHIANS 11:30

Most of us have a hard time seeing anything beautiful coming from our weaknesses! In fact, we're more likely to hide them rather than admit to them. Yet in God's hands, our weaknesses are a source of uncommon blessings.

Without weaknesses, you would have no reason to lean on God's strength, or to ask for His forgiveness. If you never needed to ask Him for forgiveness, you might never experience the depth of His love and compassion, and in turn never even glimpse God's ineffable characteristics.

An admission of weaknesses is the source of genuine humility of heart, one of the spiritual gifts God gives to those who come to Him. Your own ability to recognize your weaknesses enables you to empathize with the frailties of others and help them overcome them as a fellow traveler on the same road.

The more you think about all you have gained and learned and understood only because you can admit to being weak, the more you see just how strong, beautiful, and uncommonly blessed you really are.

Heavenly Father, show me how to use weaknesses like…

God has put into each of our lives a void
that cannot be filled by the world. We may leave
God or put Him on hold, but He is always there,
patiently waiting for us...to turn back to Him.

EMILIE BARNES

Don't we all long for a father...who cares for us
in spite of our failures? We do have that type of a father.
A father who is at His best when we are at our worst...
whose grace is strongest when our devotion is weakest.

MAX LUCADO

We know that [God] gives us every grace, every
abundant grace; and though we are so weak
of ourselves, this grace is able to carry
us through every obstacle and difficulty.

ELIZABETH ANN SETON

An Unbreakable Commitment

The eyes of the LORD range throughout the earth to strengthen those whose hearts are fully committed to him.

2 CHRONICLES 16:9

When we commit ourselves to a relationship or job, we go into it with the intention of seeing it through. But for any number of reasons, we sometimes make a decision to break our commitment.

Even spiritual commitments can fail. Sometimes we lose our resolve, or we find we have overcommitted ourselves, or we realize a particular spiritual practice is not drawing us closer to God. What then?

Unconditionally committed to you, your heavenly Father speaks no words of rejection. He has no wish to make you feel sad but only to help you grow in spiritual wisdom. The words you will most often hear from Him are "try again."

Try again with another book of devotions or a different Bible study group; change when or where you meditate and pray; adjust what you do to the time, energy, and resources God has made available to you today.

Fulfill your commitment to Him by putting your trust in His unbreakable commitment to you.

Dear God, I trust Your commitment and pledge to…

*Before anything else, above all else, beyond everything
else, God loves us. God loves us extravagantly,
ridiculously, without limit or condition.
God is in love with us...God yearns for us.*

ROBERTA BONDI

*I am not what I ought to be, I am not
what I wish to be, I am not what I hope to be;
but, by the grace of God, I am not what I was.*

JOHN NEWTON

*We walk without fear, full of hope
and courage and strength to do His will,
waiting for the endless good which He is always
giving as fast as He can get us able to take it in.*

GEORGE MACDONALD

A Powerful Friend

He saved them for His name's sake,
that He might make His mighty power known.

PSALM 106:8 NKJV

Sometimes power evokes fear. We're afraid of power that dictates or dominates, or power wielded solely for personal gain, or power exerted to rob others of power. Yet one of God's attributes is power—infinite, insurmountable, overwhelming power. Does the thought make you fearful? If so, consider for a moment what God's power means to you.

Your all-powerful God, who is not subject to the misuse of any of His attributes, is your all-powerful Friend. With Him, nothing is impossible and that's why He invites you to ask Him for anything you need or desire, believing He has the will and ability to respond to your prayers.

Because He has the power to hold you up, He encourages you to lean on Him for strength and comfort, consolation and rest. Because He alone has the power to renew and restore your spirit, He opens His arms to you and yearns to give you peace.

God's power means you need never fear anyone else's power over you, because in Him, you have an all-powerful Friend.

Lord God, grant me Your power to…

Trust in your Redeemer's strength...exercise what faith you have, and by and by [you will find] healing beneath His wings. Go from faith to faith and you shall receive blessing upon blessing.

CHARLES SPURGEON

He is the Source. Of everything. Strength for your day. Wisdom for your task. Comfort for your soul. Grace for your battle. Provision for each need. Understanding for each failure. Assistance for every encounter.

JACK HAYFORD

God's love is like a river springing up...and flowing endlessly through His creation, filling all things with life and goodness and strength.

THOMAS MERTON

*Grace is love that cares
and stoops and rescues.*

JOHN R. W. STOTT

Easy to See

Those who are wise will shine like the brightness of the heavens.

DANIEL 12:3

You might find it on the cover of a greeting card or right outside your window: in the middle of a snow-covered landscape, a bright red cardinal sits serenely on the branch of a tree. Even if you know only a little about birds, it's easy to pick out a cardinal in a winter scene!

Like a redbird against a backdrop of snow, God's beauty is clearly evident in a world marked by weakness, adversity, and troubles. His compassion stands in stark contrast to indifference, and His presence cannot be missed when He enters a heart willing to receive Him.

The work of His Spirit is nothing short of obvious too. Against a backdrop of people too busy to care, your concern for others is like a shining light in a dreary day. Your gentleness stands out when a friend needs a word of encouragement, and your everyday joy breaks through the unremitting gray of gloom and sadness.

In a winter world, it's easy to pick out the woman who has been touched by the beauty of the Lord!

Dear God, let me show more of Your…

C. S. Lewis once surmised that each person is created
to see a different facet of God's beauty—something no one
else can see in quite the same way—and then to bless
all worshipers through all eternity with
an aspect of God they could not otherwise see.

JOHN ORTBERG

God is love, and as much as I respond in allowing
myself to be transformed by that love
and acting in that love, that's my religion.

BONO

Let Jesus be in your heart,
Eternity in your spirit,
The world under your feet,
The will of God in your actions.
And let the love of God shine forth from you.

CATHERINE OF GENOA

More and More

As you continue to contemplate God's presence, you become more and more aware of His activities. You recognize Him as the source of all the things you may have taken for granted before, such as home and family, friends and coworkers, food and comforts, pleasures and gifts.

Yet God's activities don't stop there! Perhaps you have seen with your mind's eye how His hand guided you to a particular person or place at just the right time, and there you found a special blessing waiting for you. Maybe you have realized how close you came to a dangerous decision but heard Him call you back to safety. More and more, the shadows of happenstance melt away, revealing the glorious goodwill of your all-powerful God.

God sits in heaven, and He also lives in the lives of His beloved children on earth. The more you think about it, the more you want to bless Him for blessing you in all He says and does.

Dear Lord, thank You for blessing me with…

In difficulties, I can drink freely of God's power,
and experience His touch of refreshment and blessing—
much like an invigorating early spring rain.

ANABEL GILLHAM

God came to us because God wanted to join us on
the road, to listen to our story, and to help us realize that
we are not walking in circles but moving toward
the house of peace and joy. This is the great mystery...
that continues to give us comfort and consolation: we are
not alone on our journey. The God of love who gave us life
sent us [His] only Son to be with us at all times and in all
places, so that we never have to feel lost in our struggles
but always can trust that God walks with us.

HENRI J. M. NOUWEN

Blessing of His Beauty

*Grow in the grace and knowledge
of our Lord and Savior Jesus Christ.*

2 PETER 3:18

It's common to those of us who travel the same route day after day: we're so familiar with the landscape that we don't even see it anymore. When we arrive home, if someone says, "It's all over the news, and you must have passed right by the place," we sheepishly admit we did but noticed nothing out of the ordinary.

The spiritual path, too, becomes more and more familiar as you daily look to God and His will. By now you may have fallen into a routine of spiritual practices that work for you, bringing you closer to God and increasingly at ease in His presence.

At the same time, you may be seeing the same signposts over and over. The thrill of newness you experienced at the beginning has dulled to ho-hum, and the discoveries so engaging at first have slipped into the expected.

Yet amazing things are taking place. Look deeply at how God has enhanced your life with the blessing of His beauty, right where you are and through what you do every day.

Open the eyes of my spirit, Lord, to see…

God, who is love—who is, if I may say it this way,
made out of love—simply cannot help
but shed blessing on blessing upon us.

HANNAH WHITALL SMITH

Beauty puts a face on God. When we gaze at nature,
at a loved one, at a work of art, our soul immediately
recognizes and is drawn to the face of God.

MARGARET BROWNLEY

The patterns of our days are always rearranging...
and each design for living is unique,
graced with its own special beauty.

A beautiful life, a rich life, a "worthy" life is,
with God's help, in reach of every man and every woman.

C. WILLIAM FISHER

God's Good Will

Our Father in heaven, hallowed be your name, your kingdom
come, your will be done on earth as it is in heaven.

MATTHEW 6:9–10

Good mothers know this: children need clear, age-appropriate directions if they're to do what they need to do. God knows the same thing. No matter how old you are physically or spiritually, He never expects you to guess how to please Him or wonder exactly how you're supposed to follow in His way. Instead, God has given you His clear directions in the Bible, and He provides examples of how to proceed in the lives of your sisters and brothers in Christ and those who have gone before you.

God's directions are spiritually age-appropriate too. He never asks what you're not ready to give. Through His Spirit, you have received the insight and ability you need to carry out His will for you today, and He will supply you with ever-increasing wisdom as you need it to carry out His plan and purpose for your life.

He even sends reminders! Ever been prompted to extend a word of compassion and caring to a needy heart? That's God talking!

Lord, I sense that You're reminding me today to…

Guidance is a sovereign act. Not merely does God will to guide us by showing us His way.... Whatever mistakes we may make, we shall come safely home. Slippings and strayings there will be, no doubt, but the everlasting arms are beneath us; we shall be caught, rescued, restored. This is God's promise; this is how good He is. And our self-distrust, while keeping us humble, must not cloud the joy with which we lean on our faithful covenant God.

J. I. PACKER

Let your religion be less of a theory and more of a love affair.

G. K. CHESTERTON

A Place for You

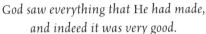

God saw everything that He had made,
and indeed it was very good.

GENESIS 1:31 NKJV

Imagine having an unlimited budget to redecorate your home! You'd surround yourself with colors, textures, and fragrances that reflect your spirit and delight your senses. You'd come up with a place both functional for you and beautiful to you.

Without constraints of any kind, God created a perfect world, both functional and beautiful. He formed the earth to provide air, water, and food for people. He shaped its hills and valleys, seas and prairies, forests and deserts as places of unparalleled magnificence. God added colors bright and startling, shaded and subtle; He showered blossoms with fragrance; He wrapped trees in engaging textures; He touched tall grasses with captivating grace.

The world around you still reflects His creative act. It's a world He made as a perfect place for you, a place He wants you to notice and enjoy and use with pleasure and thanksgiving.

A berry right off the vine, a walk through the park, a flower savored as the scent of summer—all this is the home God has created (and decorated) for you!

Lord, thank You for creating…

I am convinced that God has built into all of us
an appreciation of beauty and has even allowed us
to participate in the creation of beautiful things
and places. It may be one way God brings healing
to our brokenness, and a way that we can contribute
toward bringing wholeness to our fallen world.

MARY JANE WORDEN

God is here! I hear His voice while thrushes make
the woods rejoice. I touch His robe each time I place my
hand against a pansy's face. I breathe His breath if I but
pass verbenas trailing through the grass. God is here!
From every tree His leafy fingers beckon me.

MADELEINE AARON

From the Heart

A generous person will prosper; whoever
refreshes others will be refreshed.

PROVERBS 11:25

God's a great gift giver. One reason is He knows each recipient so intimately. But God isn't the only one who gives. Whether it's for a special occasion or as a token of affection for someone you care about, the gifts you give reflect how well you know those receiving them. Before you pick up another innocuous bouquet of flowers, think carefully about the person you're paying tribute to.

People feel honored in different ways. Some people respond best to words. For them, a card may be the most important part of a gift. Tell them how you feel verbally or in writing. Others long for the gift of your company more than one that you wrap in a box. For them, spend the day together doing something you enjoy. Others could use a break from caring for an elderly parent or need a listening ear. Give them the gift of your time and energy. Still others treasure a heartfelt hug or prayer.

Next time you're ready to give a gift, think about opening your heart before your wallet.

Lord, I desire to give the gift of…

Caring words, friendship, affectionate touch—
all of these have a healing quality. Why? Because
we were all created by God to give and receive love.

JACK FROST

Lord...give me the gift of faith to be renewed
and shared with others each day. Teach me
to live this moment only, looking neither to the past
with regret, nor the future with apprehension.
Let love be my aim and my life a prayer.

ROSEANN ALEXANDER-ISHAM

If we believe in Jesus, it is not what we gain,
but what He pours through us that counts.

OSWALD CHAMBERS

*It is always God's grace
that forms life's sweetest
spot, the softest place
to land when we want
to rest, revive, or just
revel in the fun of God's
beautiful goodness.*

JENNIFER GERELDS

Secure in Him

[God] set his seal of ownership on us, and put his Spirit in our hearts as a deposit, guaranteeing what is to come.

2 CORINTHIANS 1:22

Chances are it's happened to you. You buy something. But the moment you try to leave the store an alarm sounds. As everyone turns to look at you, you want to cry out, "Not a shoplifter!" Instead, you dutifully head back to the register so the clerk can remove the security tag attached to your purchase.

God has a security tag on you. It doesn't make an obnoxious noise if you pass a certain point or spray dye on your clothes if you try to remove it. It's more like a royal seal. God's own Spirit has marked you as His child. Your life was purchased, so to speak, by Jesus's death on the cross. He paid for the wrongs you've done, and now you're secure in His love.

Nothing can separate you from His presence, His forgiveness, or His grace. You can't be hidden from His sight or cut off from His power. You are safe and secure in His care from now until you're home with Him in heaven.

God, to me, being secure in You means...

An infinite God can give all of Himself to each of His children. He does not distribute Himself that each may have a part, but to each one He gives all of Himself as fully as if there were no others.... His love has not changed. It hasn't cooled off, and it needs no increase because He has already loved us with infinite love and there is no way that infinitude can be increased.... He is the same yesterday, today, and forever!

A. W. TOZER

Be still, and in the quiet moments, listen to the voice of your heavenly Father. His words can renew your spirit.... No one knows you and your needs like He does.

JANET L. SMITH

Confidence in Him

I trust in God, so why should I be afraid?

PSALM 56:11 NLT

Who of us hasn't, at one time or another, lacked confidence? We sometimes perceive others as being smarter, more sophisticated, or more knowledgeable than we are, and deep down inside, we wonder if we can measure up.

On our spiritual journey, the same thing can happen. Some of our fellow travelers have been lifelong Christians, talk easily about God, and know the Bible inside and out. We wonder if we could ever become so spiritually self-assured!

The Lord invites you to look at things from His perspective. When He sees you, He sees you alone. Whether your prayers come from church tradition or spring from your own heart, He treasures the sound of your voice. God's love for you is the same whether you're able to ace a graduate exam in theology or you're only beginning to explore your relationship with Him. His love is incomparable, and He compares you with no one else in the world.

When you lack confidence in yourself, He reminds you to take your confidence from Him and in His high regard for you.

Dear God, help me find my confidence in You when…

Jesus Christ has brought every need, every joy, every gratitude, every hope of ours before God. He accompanies us and brings us into the presence of God.

DIETRICH BONHOEFFER

I know that He who is far outside the whole creation takes me within Himself and hides me in His arms.... He is my heart, He is in heaven: Both there and here he shows Himself to me with equal glory.

SYMEON

Do not take over much thought for tomorrow. God, who has led you safely on so far, will lead you on to the end. Be altogether at rest in the loving holy confidence which you ought to have in His heavenly Providence.

FRANCIS DE SALES

When God Speaks

And after the fire came a gentle whisper.

1 KINGS 19:12

Have you ever had trouble hearing God's voice? It's not surprising if your answer is yes. The clatter of the world around you, as well as the clamor of your own thoughts, can muffle the clear, unmistakable sound of God speaking to you.

Once, the biblical prophet Elijah was deeply discouraged. Only after Elijah stilled the tumult of his emotions, however, could he hear God speak. In the silence of his soul, God's voice came as gently as a whisper, as tenderly as a kiss. In the stillness of his spirit, God's renewing, encouraging, and life-giving words restored him.

Today, God speaks to you softly, with gentleness and compassion. In the stillness of your spirit, He whispers words of assurance. In the quietness of your soul, He murmurs expressions of love and affection.

You won't have trouble hearing His voice when your mind—and ears—are turned to Him. And with inner distractions gone, you have the bonus of also hearing the voices of those around you.

Dear God, open my ears to hear Your voice as I…

God is not really "out there" at all. That restless heart, questioning who you are and why you were created, that quiet voice that keeps calling your name is not just out there, but dwells in you.

DAVID AND BARBARA SORENSEN

God is with us in the midst of our daily, routine lives. In the middle of cleaning the house or driving somewhere in the pickup.... Often it's in the middle of the most mundane task that He lets us know He is there with us. We realize, then, that there can be no "ordinary" moments for people who live their lives with Jesus.

MICHAEL CARD

We may ask, "Why does God bring thunderclouds and disasters when we want green pastures and still waters?" Bit by bit, we find behind the clouds the Father's feet; behind the lightning, an abiding day that has no night; behind the thunder, a still small voice that comforts with a comfort that is unspeakable.

OSWALD CHAMBERS

All in His Family

In most families, there's a relative who is rarely mentioned. Generally, this person has done something that has brought shame or embarrassment to the family.

Did you know that God's biblical family is full of embarrassments? Throughout Scripture there are accounts of liars and adulterers; tricksters and thieves; braggarts and even murderers. Yet God did not stop calling these men and women His own, and He never stopped loving them. In each case, He yearned for His loved one to return to Him.

Our heavenly Father feels the same way about the members of His family today. No matter what we have done, He longs for us to return to Him. He calls our name, loudly and clearly. He will tell anyone that we belong to Him, and even the weakest among us remains His pride and joy.

If anything holds you back from calling yourself His beloved daughter, run to Him now with it and talk to Him. You won't embarrass Him! Let your mind and heart be filled with the assurance of your place in His family today.

Dear God, the embarrassing thing I would like to overcome is…

We are forgiven and righteous because of Christ's sacrifice; therefore we are pleasing to God in spite of our failures. Christ alone is the source of our forgiveness, freedom, joy, and purpose.

ROBERT S. MCGEE

I have come to know a God who has a soft spot for rebels, who recruits people like the adulterer David, the whiner Jeremiah, the traitor Peter, and the human-rights abuser Saul of Tarsus. I have come to know a God whose Son made prodigals the heroes of his stories and the trophies of his ministry.

PHILIP YANCEY

All we are and all we have is by the...love of God! The goodness of God is infinitely more wonderful than we will ever be able to comprehend.

A. W. TOZER

A Good Question

Everyone who asks receives; he who seeks finds;
and to him who knocks, the door will be opened.

MATTHEW 7:8

Have you ever been afraid to ask a question? Perhaps you felt everyone else knew the answer, and you didn't want to sound ignorant. Chances are, however, others had the same question but were afraid to ask for the same reason. That's why, before inviting audience participation, many moderators say, "There are no stupid questions!"

God assures you of the same thing. Spiritually, there are no stupid questions. Indeed, your questions show you're thinking through what you hear from Him and about Him. Your questions reveal a desire to learn more and know more of what He has to say. All your questions are good ones to ask.

Whether your questions spring from doubt or confusion, or you're simply wondering, ask. Ask Him how to handle a sticky situation in a Christ-like manner, or how to see a current event from a godly perspective.

Find God's answer in the Bible, or talk to a mature Christian minister or friend. Ask, because a question is the beginning of wisdom.

Lord, I have a question for You...

Too many people think that finding the reason God placed us here on earth will come in one assignment with a big title and complete job description. I believe that discovering our purpose will unfold slowly, like a seed planted deep in the ground.

LYSA TERKEURST

There is a beautiful transparency to honest disciples who never wear a false face and do not pretend to be anything but who they are.

BRENNAN MANNING

God guides us, despite our uncertainties and our vagueness, even through our failings and mistakes.... He leads us step by step, from event to event. Only afterwards, as we look back over the way we have come and reconsider certain important moments in our lives in the light of all that has followed them, or when we survey the whole progress of our lives, do we experience the feeling of having been led without knowing it, the feeling that God has mysteriously guided us.

PAUL TOURNIER

It Takes Two

Have you ever asked someone to sit down with you for a private heart-to-heart? Perhaps something that person said hurt or angered you, and you want to understand. Maybe that person's recent behavior worried you, and you want to share your concerns. You're left with no hope of resolution, however, if he or she is unwilling to talk to you.

Similarly, your continuing relationship with God depends on a two-way conversation. Whenever you're burdened with doubts, especially about His love for you and His presence in your life, He urges you to sit down for a heart-to-heart with Him. He's there to listen when worries threaten to seize your thoughts and rob you of the peace you have found in Him. God wants to have an honest conversation with you when your heart is heavy with anxiety, frustration, or disappointment.

When there's a misunderstanding between you and someone else, God desires resolution. Invite the person for a heart-to-heart. When there's a misunderstanding between you and God, go ahead and sit down, because He's already there, waiting for you.

Dear God, I want to talk with You about…

Lord, hear my prayer. When I stumble over my words,
or when I can't find the right words to say,
listen to my heart. I want to talk with You. I want
to walk with You. Hear me, Lord, and answer
with grace and love and mercy. Take my hand
and my heart and lead me in prayer. Amen.

MARILYN JANSEN

To believe in God starts with a conclusion
about Him, develops into confidence in Him,
and then matures into a conversation with Him.

STUART BRISCOE

He walks with me, and he talks with me,
and he tells me I am his own.
And the joy we share as we tarry there
none other has ever known.

C. AUSTIN MILES

Instead of filling with expectations, the joy-filled expect nothing—and are filled. This breath! This oak tree! This daisy! This work! This sky! These people! This place! This day! Surprise!

ANN VOSKAMP

Mercy Me

Who is a God like you, who pardons sin and forgives
the transgression of the remnant of his inheritance?
You do not stay angry forever but delight to show mercy.

MICAH 7:18

Throwing yourself on the mercy of the court may sound romantic in a fictional courtroom drama. But what it actually means is that a client hopes that by telling the judge the story behind what happened, the judge will exercise compassion and excuse laws that have been broken due to extenuating circumstances. The client is guilty. That part is clear. It's the sentence that's up in the air.

God extends His mercy to you whether there are extenuating circumstances or not. You're guilty, but declared not guilty. Any sentence you would have received, Jesus has taken on Himself. The final judgment is freedom.

Suppose someone then commits an offense against you. If God's compassion has made a true difference in your heart, mercy will influence how you respond. You'll offer what you've received…kindness, forgiveness, and freedom. The truth is, God's the only true judge. Extend mercy to others and let God handle the rest.

God, some of the ways I can extend mercy are…

Trust the past to the mercy of God, the present
to His love, and the future to His Providence.

AUGUSTINE

Grace comes free of charge to people who do not deserve
it, and I am one of those people.... Now I am trying
in my own small way to pipe the tune of grace. I do so
because I know, more surely than I know anything,
that any pang of healing or forgiveness or goodness
I have ever felt comes solely from the grace of God.

PHILIP YANCEY

Love is an act of endless forgiveness,
a tender look that becomes a habit.

PETER USTINOV

Faith of a Child

Jesus said, "Let the little children come to Me,
and do not forbid them; for of such is the kingdom of heaven."

MATTHEW 19:14 NKJV

God has a way of turning our ideas upside down. During the Lord's earthly ministry, He embraced children, praised them, and pointed to them as examples for grown-ups to follow in the way of faith!

Childlike faith is open and trusting, innocent of doubt and deceit. It is also teachable, eager to hear more and discover more about our heavenly Father. This is the kind of faith God would have you emulate, no matter how many candles might crowd your birthday cake this year.

As your relationship with God grows, your faith will also grow if you remain open to hearing what He has to say. Your faith matures as you put your trust in Him in more areas of your life. You'll desire to follow Him in ever-expanding ways. The more of your life you surrender, the more childlike your faith becomes!

The next time the innocent eyes of a small child look up to you, imagine yourself looking to your heavenly Father with the innocent eyes of a childlike faith.

Lord, help me surrender in the area of...

Love loves to be told what it knows already....
It wants to be asked for what it longs to give.

PETER TAYLOR FORSYTH

He knows you work hard. He knows you give your
all but sometimes come up short. He knows when
you're worn out by life and feel faint in your faith.
God understands when you feel like crawling into a hole
or plopping down in defeat. When you feel like you've
endured one too many losses, God wants you to simply
put your hand in His—and trust. He promises
to exchange His strength for your weariness.

A Double Freedom

*The Lord is the Spirit, and where
the Spirit of the Lord is, there is freedom.*

2 CORINTHIANS 3:17

Though many are afraid a relationship with God would limit them, the opposite is true. The more you learn about God, the more you find Him a God of two freedoms: freedom *from* and freedom *to*. If you have one without the other, you're living with only half the freedom God has in mind for you!

God's first freedom is freedom from those things that would disturb your spirit—things like fear and guilt, sadness and despondency, hopelessness and despair. In Him, you possess the light of His presence to scatter shadows of mind and heart and the reality of His love to release you from anything that would threaten your spiritual serenity.

God's second freedom is freedom to make peace with your past, knowing that your new life has begun in Him. You're free to take delight in the present moment, which opens you to the blessings, opportunities, and miracles around you. And no matter who would tell you differently, in Him you're free to look forward to the future with God-given hope and confidence.

Lord, I thank You for my freedom from and to...

Peace of conscience, liberty of heart, the sweetness
of abandoning ourselves in the hands of God,
the joy of always seeing the light grow in our hearts,
finally, freedom from the fears and insatiable desires
of the times, multiply a hundredfold the happiness
which the true children of God possess in the midst
of their [trials] if they are faithful.

FRANÇOIS DE FÉNELON

We walk without fear, full of hope
and courage and strength to do His will,
waiting for the endless good which He is always
giving as fast as He can get us able to take it in.

GEORGE MACDONALD

Answer to Prayer

Show kindness and mercy to one another.

ZECHARIAH 7:9 ESV

To someone who knows little about God's ways with His people, answers to prayer must seem like little more than wishful thinking. So even though you may appreciate the dependability and wisdom of God's answers, you may find yourself hesitant to recommend prayer to a particular friend.

Instead, you opt to sit down with her and listen while she pours out her words to you. Through your gestures and responses, you let her know you empathize with her and with everything she's going through. Then you might gently share with her the Spirit-nourished thoughts of your heart. If the time feels right, you might invite her to listen as you lift up her needs and desires to God.

In doing so, you're extending God's caring and goodness, kindness and love to someone who has yet to learn about the power of prayer. She won't recognize that God heard the prayer she didn't even know how to offer, but His answer was sitting right across the table from her. His answer to an unspoken prayer was you.

Lord, teach me how to respond to the needs of others, especially…

I would rather make mistakes in kindness
and compassion than work miracles
in unkindness and hardness.

MOTHER TERESA

The wonder of our Lord is that He is so accessible
to us in the common things of our lives: the cup of water...
breaking of the bread...welcoming children into
our arms...fellowship over a meal...giving thanks.
A simple attitude of caring, listening,
and lovingly telling the truth.

NANCIE CARMICHAEL

To pray is to change. This is a great grace.
How good of God to provide a path whereby
our lives can be taken over by love and joy and peace
and patience and kindness and goodness
and faithfulness and gentleness and self-control.

RICHARD J. FOSTER

No Experience Possible

Samuel answered, "Speak, for Your servant hears."

1 SAMUEL 3:10 NKJV

If you have ever applied for a job, the interviewer probably asked about your work history. She wanted to know what experience you could bring to the company and how much further training you might need to fill the vacant position.

When you approach God, however, one thing's for sure: He won't spend time asking about your qualifications. Why? Because spiritual qualities come from His Spirit, and you practice them as you are enabled by Him to grow in spiritual experience and maturity. With God, no experience is necessary because there's no earthly experience possible to prepare you for the spiritual position He has in mind for you.

There's one thing, though, that God would ask of you, and that's to undergo spiritual training. Just as on-the-job training prepares you for the tasks of the position, so in-the-Spirit training gets you ready for your responsibilities in God's family. These are to model His qualities, to reflect His beauty, and to radiate His peace.

For His beloved child, it's not only a job for a lifetime, but the job of a lifetime!

Dear God, thank You for the in-the-Spirit training that I am receiving from...

This is what the past is for! Every experience God gives us, every person He puts in our lives is the perfect preparation for the future that only He can see.

CORRIE TEN BOOM

Nothing that happens to me is meaningless, and that it is good for us all that it should be so, even if it runs counter to our own wishes…. I'm here for some purpose, and I only hope I may fulfill it.

DIETRICH BONHOEFFER

Whenever, wherever, however You want me, I'll go. And I'll begin this very minute. Lord, as I stand up from this place, and as I take my first step forward, will You consider this is a step toward complete obedience to You? I'll call it the step of yes.

BROTHER ANDREW

So let us come boldly
to the throne of our
gracious God. There we
will receive his mercy,
and we will find grace
to help us when
we need it most.

HEBREWS 4:16 NLT

His Effective Gifts

Each man has his own gift from God;
one has this gift, another has that.

1 CORINTHIANS 7:7

Where women and men with diversity of talents and skills contribute to the overall good, corporations, communities, and households thrive. People bringing their strengths together accomplish more than any one of them could alone, and with far more effectiveness.

When you entered your relationship with God, you brought with you certain skills, talents, interests, and abilities. These are exactly the gifts He will use for the good and well-being of His family, your spiritual sisters and brothers. Whether your particular gifts have brought you prominence in the world or are generally unnoticed by others, God sees them and holds them in high esteem.

God the Creator has blessed you with gifts needed by and necessary to His family right now where you are. He may call you to work alongside someone else to lighten the common burden, or He may direct you to a unique task only you have the ability to do. However it turns out, you may be surprised how effectively He uses you—and how great you'll feel inside!

Dear God, please show me what gifts I can contribute when...

In the endless cycle of grace,
He gives us gifts to serve the world.

ANN VOSKAMP

The secret of life is that all we have
and are is a gift of grace to be shared.

LLOYD JOHN OGILVIE

When I stand before God at the end of my life,
I would hope that I would not have a single bit of talent
left, and could say, "I used everything you gave me."

ERMA BOMBECK

Use what talents you possess: the woods would be very
silent if no birds sang there except those that sang best.

HENRY VAN DYKE

The Dirty Details

Those who guards their mouths and their
tongues keep themselves from calamity.

PROVERBS 21:23

You've just heard a delicious piece of gossip.

Your next steps are what count with God. First, you might say that you'll remember the person in your prayers. Now the conversation has shifted from the shadows of secrecy to the light of genuine caring.

Second, consider whether or not the information you've heard is true, and if it is true, whether or not you need to repeat it. The Holy Spirit provides good counsel for questions like this because the reputation of another child of God is at stake.

Third, implement your God-given judgment by doing the kindest thing you can. Sometimes kindness lies in speaking of the matter in the best terms possible in keeping with the truth; at other times, in remaining silent. What you say or don't say lightens the burden of gossip for another person and heightens the respect others hold for us.

The next time you hear all the dirty details, respond with God's Spirit of kindness, truth, and love. After all, this is how He responds to you every day.

Dear God, guard my tongue and help me to...

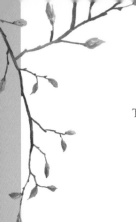

Three things in human life are important:
the first is to be kind; the second is to be kind;
and the third is to be kind.

HENRY JAMES

When you are in the dark, listen,
and God will give you a very precious message
for someone else when you get into the light.

OSWALD CHAMBERS

One taper lights a thousand,
Yet shines as it has shone;
And the humblest light may kindle
One brighter than its own.

HEZEKIAH BUTTERWORTH

As our love for the Lord increases and our knowledge
of His Word deepens, we have more to offer
the body of Christ.... That's why Paul urges
us to press on, show up, keep going.

LIZ CURTIS HIGGS

Keep On Practicing

Let's not get tired of doing what is good.

GALATIANS 6:9 NLT

Practice makes perfect." We've heard it said, usually by mothers or teachers urging us as children to try again at the piano or free throw line. As adults, we may have used the same words ourselves to encourage kids to not give up.

If you're ever discouraged in your spiritual journey, you might hear "practice makes perfect" whispered in the recesses of your heart. That's God's Spirit reminding you not to let a bad day or an off moment turn you away from practicing spiritual values and principles. Do not give up simply because you lost your temper, said words you wish you could take back, or neglected to do what you knew was right. When that happens, practice going to God in prayer and asking His forgiveness. It will be yours.

Then, get right back to practicing the beautiful strains of His love in your life. Your growing proficiency becomes unmistakable, and before you know it, your practice yields life-changing results.

Remember, practice comes before perfect—and perfect will come when you're standing with Him in heaven.

Dear Lord, I want to be more practiced at…

The beauty of grace—our only permanent
deliverance from guilt—is that it meets us where
we are and gives us what we don't deserve.

CHARLES R. SWINDOLL

For God is, indeed, a wonderful Father who longs
to pour out His mercy upon us, and whose majesty
is so great that He can transform us from deep within.

TERESA OF AVILA

The abundant life that Jesus talked about begins
with the unfathomable Good News put simply:
My dear child, I love you anyway.

ALICE CHAPIN

Be assured, if you walk with Him and look to Him
and expect help from Him, He will never fail you.

GEORGE MUELLER

Privilege of Prayer

The prayer of a righteous person is powerful and effective.

JAMES 5:16

For no particular reason, a person's name pops into your mind. You wake up in the small hours of the morning burdened by the plight of people in a faraway land. To many women and men of God, these seemingly random thoughts prompt a call to prayer.

God desires to hear you asking Him to bless your friends, loved ones, and causes you care about. Sometimes, however, He may invite you to pray for someone you haven't seen for a while, someone you barely know, or even a stranger you met only in passing. Through the stirrings of His Spirit, God brings to mind a situation pleading for your heartfelt prayer.

God builds in you a source of power—power to make a difference. Just as His words called the world and everything in it into being, so your God-inspired words continue His creative work among people. Your prayers, spoken according to His will, put you in partnership with Him as He comforts and cares for, leads and guides, lifts and saves fearful and endangered hearts.

Dear God, I pray for…

When you come into the presence of God, He draws near to you to listen to what is on your heart. Delighting in your presence, He hushes the heavenly host to hear the petitions you bring. And pleased with every indication of your increasing trust, He receives your praise and gratitude, responding in Spirit with peace and joy.

God shall be my hope, my stay,
my guide and lantern to my feet.

WILLIAM SHAKESPEARE

Do you believe that God is near? He wants you to. He wants you to know that He is in the midst of your world. Wherever you are as you read these words, He is present. In your car. On the plane. In your office, your bedroom, your den. He's near. And He is more than near. He is active.

MAX LUCADO

Design of Wholeness

We are the clay, you are the potter;
we are all the work of your hand.

ISAIAH 64:8

Even if you don't do needlework yourself, you may still appreciate the stunning creations of those who do. Indeed, women throughout the ages have excelled in the art of bringing simple strands of thread together to a complete and pleasing whole.

A rainbow's range of colors goes into most needlework projects, but until the design is finished, the creator doesn't know for sure what it will look like. She begins with the hope it will come out as planned, and she proceeds on faith.

Consider the many and various threads of your life—self, spirit, family, friends, work, service. Each day, your words and actions weave them together, but you don't know what your completed picture will look like. God assures you, however, of this: it will be beautiful, because His Spirit blesses every strand of your life with His goodness and truth.

As you extend your hands to others in love, friendship, and service, the threads of His love create a stunning design. Chances are, those around you are already admiring it!

Lord, I'm beginning to see a design take shape in...

The Lord doesn't waste anything we've been through, least of all the painful bits. He uses them all, to shape our hearts and to help others.

LIZ CURTIS HIGGS

Those who never rebelled against God or at some point in their lives shaken their fists in the face of heaven, have never encountered God at all.

CATHERINE MARSHALL

Jesus is the Savior, but He is even more than that!
He is more than a forgiver of our sins.
He is even more than our Provider of eternal life—
He is our Redeemer! He is the One who is ready
to recover and restore what the power of sin
and death has taken from us.

JACK HAYFORD

Just in Time

You may be familiar with the just-in-time business model. Under a just-in-time plan, managers strive to produce merchandise at the same rate their customers order it. They want to avoid the expense of holding excess product, yet remain able to meet demand. Ideally, the process provides businesses and customers with what they need when they need it.

In many ways, God sends His blessings into our lives in a just-in-time process. He is the provider of everything we need or will ever need, though He does not give it to us all at once. We would be overwhelmed if He did! Yet He will never withhold from us what we need, nor is He ever slow in providing it.

God's just-in-time plan for you is twofold. First, it leads you to ask Him for your daily needs. Second, it prompts you to trust Him to meet your future needs. Yes, He knows what they are (even better than you do!), but He desires to hear your requests.

God will be there just in time for you—every time.

Today, Lord, I come before You to request…

God longs to give favor—that is, spiritual strength
and health—to those who seek Him, and Him alone.
He grants spiritual favors and victories, not because
the one who seeks Him is holier than anyone else,
but in order to make His holy beauty
and His great redeeming power known.

TERESA OF AVILA

God promises to keep us in the palm of [His] hand,
with or without our awareness. God has already made
a space for us, even if we have not made a space for God.

DAVID AND BARBARA SORENSEN

God has a wonderful plan for each person He has chosen.
He knew even before He created this world what beauty
He would bring forth from our lives.

LOUISE B. WYLY

*G*od is looking for people who will come in simple dependence upon His grace, and rest in simple faith upon His greatness. At this very moment, He's looking at you.

JACK HAYFORD

The Beauty of It

I the LORD *do not change.*

MALACHI 3:6

Most of us freely admit it—we're not always consistent in word and action, or in mood and emotion.

God makes no such claim because He's a God of perfect consistency. He never varies in temperament or attitude. Promises He made to people long ago apply to you today, and what He said in the past was true then and is true now and will be true in the future.

How comforting to know that the compassion God feels for you right now is the compassion He will feel for you tomorrow too. The arms He holds out to you at this moment are the same arms that will open to you whenever you reach out for His tender embrace. His ear, bent to hear you today, always will be there for you.

Your God is not subject to variation. Despite the changes that ever have or ever will take place in your life, His love for you will never change. That's the beauty of it.

Lord, enable me to show consistency in my love for...

May the Lord direct your hearts into the love
of God and into the steadfastness of Christ.

2 THESSALONIANS 3:5 NASB

It is God to whom and with whom we travel,
and while He is the End of our journey,
He is also at every stopping place.

ELISABETH ELLIOT

Regardless of whether we feel strong or weak
in our faith, we remember that our assurance is not
based upon our ability to conjure up some special feeling.
Rather, it is built upon a confident assurance
in the faithfulness of God. We focus on His
trustworthiness and especially on His steadfast love.

RICHARD J. FOSTER

God never abandons anyone on whom
He has set His love; nor does Christ,
the good shepherd, ever lose track of His sheep.

J. I. PACKER

A Different View

Blessed are your eyes for they see, and your ears for they hear.

MATTHEW 13:16 NKJV

Your circumstances may not have changed over the course of your life. But even if they haven't, it's a good chance you find yourself viewing things differently than you did in the past. It's bound to happen when you look at the world through spiritual eyes.

Your life continues to have good things in it, but now you recognize them as blessings from God. You enjoy them more, because you know whom to thank. Worry about keeping them forever? No, because your eyes are not on the gifts, but on the Giver.

In the same way, your life continues to have things in it you wish you could change. But now they serve not to bring you down, but to lift you up to God as you lean on Him for courage and strength. Despair about the future? No, because your focus is not on your power, but on His.

What a difference in how things look when they're seen from a believing heart! And this is the kind of difference people need to hear about. It's a different view you can help them see.

Lord, one thing I see differently now is…

Faith allows us to continually delight in life
since we have placed our needs in God's hands.

JANET L. SMITH

There are no hidden reserves in the promises of God that
are meant to deprive them of their complete fulfillment.

HANNAH WHITALL SMITH

There is an activity of the Spirit, silent, unseen,
which must be the dynamic of any form of truly creative,
fruitful trust. When we commit a predicament,
a possibility, a person to God in genuine confidence,
we do not merely step aside and tap our foot until
God comes through. We remain involved. We remain
in contact with God in gratitude and praise.

EUGENIA PRICE

Victory's in Sight

With God we will gain the victory.

PSALM 60:12

You are victorious. God reminds you of this truth through Scripture, as well as through His Spirit as you pray. His whisper confirms it in your heart. But victory isn't all fireworks, parades, and cheers from an appreciative crowd. It's about overcoming. Unfortunately, that means it requires some obstacle to overcome.

It may be hard to see your life as victorious in the face of failure, disappointment, or continued conflict, but every war that's ever been fought was won through a series of battles. Not every individual battle will be victorious. What matters is how it turns out in the end.

Is a major conflict raging in your life? A rebellious child, chronic illness, the loss of a job, a betrayal by someone you love… whatever your struggle, both you and God are on the battlefield. Even if victory doesn't seem close at hand, God is. Your fight is also His. Be strategic and courageous in pursuing the right course. Don't let discouragement tempt you to give up. Today's skirmish may be the decisive battle that wins the war.

God, to me real victory looks like…

I trust You always though I may seem to be lost and in the shadow of death. I will not fear, for You are ever with me. And You will never leave me to face my perils alone.

THOMAS MERTON

Grace is not simply leniency when we have sinned. Grace is the enabling gift of God not to sin. Grace is power, not just pardon.

JOHN PIPER

God still draws near to us in the ordinary, commonplace, everyday experiences and places.... He comes in surprising ways.

HENRY GARIEPY

Combat comes before victory. If God has chosen special trials for you to endure, be assured He has kept a very special place in His heart just for you. A badly bruised soul is one who is chosen.

L. B. COWMAN

Prayer for the Prodigal

[Jesus said,] "In the same way, I tell you, there is rejoicing in the presence of the angels of God over one sinner who repents."

LUKE 15:10

What do you do with a wayward child? If you love her, you refuse to turn your back on her. You're patient with her but continue to set boundaries. You allow her to experience the consequences of her own actions, so she'll understand the benefit of changing her ways. You celebrate her victories and hold her close when she fails. You tell her you love her, even if she claims to hate you. You never give up.

Are you that wayward child? Even if you view yourself as a good girl, you can still nurture rebellion in your life. God will never give up on you, even if you've given up on yourself. That doesn't mean He won't challenge you to change. God's love is strong enough to comfort and confront.

If the wayward child is yours, take heart. God's at work. Lean on Him for the wisdom to comfort or confront. There's always hope. It's not what you're hoping for, but who your hope is in, that makes the difference.

God, my definition of hope is...

It is God's will that we believe that we see Him
continually, though it seems to us that the sight
be only partial; and through this belief He makes us
always to gain more grace, for God wishes to be seen,
and He wishes to be sought, and He wishes to be expected,
and He wishes to be trusted.

JULIAN OF NORWICH

Whoso draws nigh to God
One step through doubtings dim,
God will advance a mile
In blazing light to him.

Faith is the daring of the soul
to go farther than it can see.

WILLIAM NEWTON CLARKE

Time to Be Kind

Try to do good to each other and to all people.

1 THESSALONIANS 5:15 NLT

In the dictionary, the word "kind" is described as an attribute of someone who gives pleasure or relief. What a beautiful picture of how God treats us. Would God, and those who know you best, use the same word to describe you?

You can give pleasure or relief without knowing someone well. You can offer a cold bottle of water to the teen selling magazines door-to-door in the summer heat. You can compliment a stranger on how beautiful she looks. But the better you know people, the better able you'll be to extend acts of kindness that do more than brighten someone's day. Those acts have the power to encourage a weary heart.

Why not schedule a surprise massage for a new mom and babysit her newborn? Reach out to a friend on the anniversary of a loved one's death? Use your experience to help a new grad assemble her first resume?

Creativity and kindness are great partners. Ask God to help you better see others' needs. Then seek innovative ways to provide pleasure or relief.

God, I want to be kind. Teach me to…

A happy life is made up of little things...
a gift sent, a letter written, a call made...
a cake made, a book lent, a check sent.

CAROL HOLMES

He is in me, perfection, and His Spirit
is intertwined with mine.... He is maturing me slowly,
gently, with His kindness and compassion.

SARAH MAE

Look deep within yourself and recognize what brings
life and grace into your heart. It is this that can be
shared with those around you. You are loved by God.
This is an inspiration to love.

CHRISTOPHER DE VINCK

One Thing Leads to Another

This is what the Lord *Almighty says:*
"Give careful thought to your ways."

HAGGAI 1:5

Mouse Trap was a popular kids' game in the sixties. Kids would construct a trap out of plastic wheels, tubes, funnels, and slides. When complete, they'd release a metal ball that would roll, tumble, and twirl from piece to piece until finally lowering a cage that would catch a plastic mouse.

Everything you do is like one plastic piece of a Mouse Trap game. It interacts with something or someone else. Choosing paper or plastic at the grocery store affects the environment in different ways. Choosing a kind word over a harsh one affects the direction of your relationships. Choosing to follow God or your own fickle feelings affects the heart of the woman you're becoming day-by-day.

Living intentionally means living thoughtfully and prayerfully. It means considering more than what feels good, looks good, or seems harmless right now. It means taking the future into consideration—so you don't wind up being the one caught in a trap. Decisions have consequences, short-term and long-term, positive or negative. Ask God for the wisdom you need each day to put the right piece into place.

God, help me evaluate the long-term impact of…

To make the best use of your life, you must never forget two truths: First, compared with eternity, life is extremely brief. Second, earth is only a temporary residence. You won't be here long, so don't get too attached.

RICK WARREN

We are His only witnesses. God is counting on each of us. No angel has been given the job. We are the lanterns—Christ is the light inside.

OLETA SPRAY

Spiritual strongholds begin with a thought. One thought becomes a consideration. A consideration develops into an attitude, which leads then to action. Action repeated becomes a habit, and a habit establishes a "power base for the enemy," that is, a stronghold.

ELISABETH ELLIOT

All those who live with
any degree of serenity live
by some assurance of grace.

REINHOLD NIEBUHR

Finding Solace in Solitude

[Jesus] went out to the mountain to pray,
and continued all night in prayer to God.

LUKE 6:12 NKJV

You weren't created to live a solitary life. God designed you to love and be loved. But sometimes finding a quiet place where you can be by yourself is exactly what you need. Jesus needed it. He often headed off to a solitary place. Sometimes it was a mountaintop. Other times it was a garden. That doesn't mean Jesus was alone. Jesus sought a secluded spot so He could spend some one-on-one time with His heavenly Father.

Jesus sought solitude when He heard John the Baptist had been killed. He took time out when crowds of needy people kept Him so busy that He couldn't find time to eat. And right before He was arrested, Jesus was having a heart-to-heart discussion with His Father in an olive grove.

Anytime you're overwhelmed, follow Jesus's example. Take a walk or head to a park bench. If you have small children, head into the closet or the bathroom and close the door for a minute or two. God's there in the silence, waiting to quiet your heart.

God, a solitary spot where I'd like to meet with You is...

You know how it feels when you're in love
with somebody and you long to be with that person?
God wants us to feel that way about Him.

STORMIE OMARTIAN

Moses does not encounter the living God at the mall.
He finds Him (or is found by Him) somewhere out
in the deserts of Sinai, a long way from the comforts
of Egypt.... Where did the great prophet Elijah
go to recover his strength? To the wild.
As did John the Baptist, and his cousin, Jesus,
who is led by the Spirit into the wilderness.

JOHN ELDREDGE

Down and Out

Do not let your hearts be troubled.
You believe in God; believe also in me.

JOHN 14:1

A traffic sign reading DIP provides advance warning of a depression in the road. Unfortunately, life doesn't come with bright yellow signs. Sometimes, things like depression catch you by surprise.

Everyone faces sadness on the road of life. It's natural to feel sad when facing a significant loss or traumatic event. But sometimes those feelings won't go away or they show up when life seems to be moving along just fine. If this happens, openly sharing your feelings with God is important. So is doing all you can to make positive, healthy choices and changes in your life.

But suppose these feelings still won't let up. If sleep begins to elude you, you find it hard to concentrate, you begin to gain or lose weight, you feel hopeless, worthless, or suicidal, call on God—but call on others as well. Depression is more than just melancholy. It doesn't show a lack of faith to ask for outside help when you need it. A doctor or counselor may be the answer God's providing to your prayers.

God, today I'm feeling…

God has given each of you some special abilities;
be sure to use them to help each other, passing on to others
God's many kinds of blessings.

1 PETER 4:10 TLB

Hope begins in the dark, the stubborn hope that if you
just show up and try to do the right thing, the dawn will
come. You wait and watch and work: You don't give up.

ANNE LAMOTT

The loving God we serve has immeasurable compassion
and tenderness toward each of us throughout our lives.

JAMES DOBSON

Identity Theft

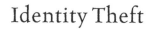

*God sent the Spirit of His Son into our hearts,
the Spirit who calls out, "Abba, Father."*

GALATIANS 4:6

Many people have become victims of identity theft. Perhaps you're one of them. You didn't hold tightly to your identity and somewhere along the way, it was lost. Perhaps in a tempting moment, you surrendered your identity for something that looked more fun, more interesting. You forgot you were a child of God.

You neglected to call your Father. You didn't read the love letters He'd written. You figured you'd strike out on your own. After all, picking up another identity was easy enough. All you had to do was blend in with the crowd. Maybe you did a few things you were ashamed of. At times, you considered calling home but figured it was too late. You'd made your choice. You were no longer the person you'd been before.

The truth is, your identity can never be lost or stolen. The Bible says God's Spirit holds it safe throughout eternity. Once God's called you His child, you can never be anything else. Your identity and destiny are secure. Even if you turn your back on God, He'll never turn His back on you. The reach of His enduring love will always lead you home.

God, being Your child means…

Almighty God seeks to redeem each of us. He stoops low. He comes as the incarnate Jesus, lays down His life, and then sends His Spirit to help, heal, strengthen, and rebuild the personalities of those He has redeemed.

JACK HAYFORD

Peace of conscience, liberty of heart, the sweetness of abandoning ourselves in the hands of God, the joy of always seeing the light grow in our hearts, finally, freedom from the fears and insatiable desires of the times, multiply a hundredfold the happiness which the true children of God possess in the midst of their [trials], if they are faithful.

FRANÇOIS DE FÉNELON

God's There When You Grieve

As one whom his mother comforts, so I will comfort you.

ISAIAH 66:13 ESV

God grieves. He understands the anguish of being separated from someone you love. That's why Jesus sacrificed His life, so that death wouldn't be a final good-bye. Jesus's death paid the price for our rebellion and opened the gates of heaven. Now we have the assurance of being with God throughout eternity.

But what about our grief, the profound emptiness we feel when someone we love crosses from this life into the next? Yes, God's assurance of heaven remains steadfast for those who love Him. But what about us, the ones left behind?

Everyone grieves as uniquely as they live. People can give you advice on what helped them in their time of need. They can comfort you with kindness and prayer or reach out to help in practical ways. But only God can heal the sorrow you feel. His gifts of peace, comfort, and compassion may feel elusive at times. But remember, feelings don't paint an accurate picture of the truth. Keep reaching out to Him, even when tears are all you have to offer.

God, today I ask for Your comfort for…

If you are seeking after God, you may be sure of this:
God is seeking you much more. He is the lover,
and you are His beloved. He has promised Himself to you.

JOHN OF THE CROSS

Let my soul take refuge...beneath the shadow
of Your wings: let my heart, this sea of restless waves,
find peace in You, O God.

AUGUSTINE

In the blackest, God is closest, at work, forging
His perfect and right will. Though it is black and we can't
see and our world seems to be free-falling and we feel
utterly alone, Christ is most present to us.

ANN VOSKAMP

The Attitude of Aging

Even when I am old and gray, do not forsake me,
My God, till I declare your power to the next generation,
your might to all who are to come.

PSALM 71:18

What comes to mind when you think about getting older? Wrinkles, body ailments, or, if you're a woman, perhaps the benefits of an eighteen-hour bra? Or wisdom, experience, and freedom from the pressure to be fashion forward? The kind of person you'll grow up and grow old to be depends a lot on the attitude you bring to each season of life.

Society may not fully value those who're considered over the hill as much as those still climbing it, but we can. We know God does. In the Bible, we read how He invited Moses, Abraham, and Sarah to do amazing things when they were well past their prime. Who knows what God has in store for you?

God says He numbers our days. We don't know why some die young and others live to celebrate the century mark. What we do know is that getting older is a privilege. Each new day and every season is a gift. Accept them with open arms.

God, one attitude about aging I need Your help changing is…

If you're looking at 30 and you're scared, you still got it.
If you're looking at 40 and you're scared, you still got it....
If you're 50, 60, 70, 80, God still has something for you....
Something you are uniquely called and equipped to do.

LIZ CURTIS HIGGS

Dreams carried around in one's heart for years,
if they are dreams that have God's approval,
have a way of suddenly materializing.

CATHERINE MARSHALL

All the way to heaven is heaven begun
to the Christian who walks near enough
to God to hear the secrets He has to impart.

E. M. BOUNDS

Great Expectations

Blessed are those who mourn, for they will be comforted.

MATTHEW 5:4

You know exactly how everything's going to turn out. You've pictured it in your mind a thousand times. Then the unexpected happens. Reality paints a totally different picture than the one you'd hoped and prayed for, leaving you bewildered and discouraged. How do you keep moving forward when you're headed in a direction you never imagined you'd go?

Jesus's followers knew this kind of disappointment. For centuries the Jews anticipated a Messiah, someone akin to a king, who would bring the Jewish people back to the height of political power. Then came Jesus. Not only was He a different kind of Savior than they were expecting, He was arrested and crucified. Talk about discouraging news! But God's plan was better than anything the Jews ever imagined. Jesus arose from the dead, bringing the power of God's Spirit and the promise of forgiveness to everyone, not just the Jews.

When disappointment leaves you discouraged, remember God has something better in mind. Trade your heartache for anticipation as you wait for the beauty of God's plan to unfold.

Lord, please give me a new vision to replace my discouragement over…

We know that love is not the absence of pain.
If anything, love is the promise of pain. No one has
loved more deeply than God. Has anyone ever been more
betrayed? God would not know suffering if He did not
know love. But because He is Love, He chose to suffer on
our behalf. Without love there is no glory in suffering.

ERWIN MCMANUS

Every time Jesus sees that there is a possibility of giving
us more than we know how to ask for, He does so.

OLE HALLESBY

We are made to reach out beyond our grasp.

OSWALD CHAMBERS

Along comes this idea called grace to upend all that "as you reap, so you will sow" stuff. Grace defies reason and logic. Love interrupts, if you like, the consequences of your actions, which...is very good news indeed.

BONO

When Teardrops Fall

He will wipe every tear from their eyes.
There will be no more death or mourning or crying or pain,
for the old order of things has passed away.

REVELATION 21:4

They show up when you're joyful. They flow when you hear bad news. They appear when you're angry, when your hormones are on the rampage, when you pray, or sometimes, for what seems like absolutely no reason at all. Tears can be a nuisance. But no matter how hard you try, it's tough to keep them inside when they're crying to get out.

It can feel uncomfortable to cry, especially in front of others, because it's such an intimate act. It reveals there's something going on inside that runs deeper than words can express. The Bible says that God keeps every one of your tears in a bottle. He knows when and why each one falls. He doesn't consider crying weak or unnecessary. After all, Jesus wept when His friend Lazarus died, even though He was about to raise Him from the dead.

God promises that one day, tears will be a thing of the past. Until then, picture Him drying your tears. What breaks your heart breaks His.

God, when I'm brokenhearted, help me remember…

God walks with us.... He scoops us up in His arms
or simply sits with us in silent strength until
we cannot avoid the awesome recognition
that yes, even now, He is here.

GLORIA GAITHER

Trust the past to the mercy of God, the present
to His love, and the future to His Providence.

AUGUSTINE

Praise God for His faithfulness. Though we are
seldom ready when tragedy strikes,
He is already there, prepared to help us, to heal us.

LIZ CURTIS HIGGS

I have learned that faith means trusting in advance
what will only make sense in reverse.

PHILIP YANCEY

Staying Grounded

I do believe; help me overcome my unbelief!

MARK 9:24

Once upon a time, people believed the world was flat, the sun revolved around the earth, and mermaids were demonic creatures who seduced sailors in order to steal their souls. Over the years, myths have been debunked, and science has set our solar system straight. But that doesn't mean we hold the answers to every mystery of life.

When it comes to God, faith and doubt often go hand in hand. That's because it's hard to gather concrete evidence about someone we can't see, hear, or touch. Of course, we don't have to totally understand how gravity works to believe it's real. And the same is true with God.

Don't allow doubts or unanswered questions to construct a myth about who God is and what He's like. Rest in God's millennia-long track record of loving faithfulness by reading accounts of people just like you as recorded in the Bible. Keep a journal of how you've seen God at work in your life. Then reread your own faith journey whenever doubts arise. God, like gravity, will keep you grounded.

God, please put my doubts to rest about…

*What is faith? It is the confident assurance
that something we want is going to happen.
It is the certainty that what we hope for is waiting for us,
even though we cannot see it up ahead.*

HEBREWS 11:1 TLB

*When a train goes through a tunnel and it gets dark,
you don't throw away the ticket and jump off.
You sit still and trust the engineer.*

CORRIE TEN BOOM

*We do not know how this is true—
where would faith be if we did?—but we do know
that all things that happen are full of shining seed.
Light is sown for us—not darkness.*

Picture Perfect

*How good and pleasant it is when
God's people live together in unity!*

PSALM 133:1

A puzzle is a great example of unity. Each distinctive piece interlocks with those around it. Together, they form a picture that can only be seen when every piece is in its proper place.

God calls His children to be "one" in Him. But unity doesn't equal uniformity. At times, this causes division. One woman raises her hands while singing in church. Another doesn't feel comfortable being that demonstrative. She may feel the first woman is distracting or even believe she's doing something God wouldn't approve of. Soon, the two have their eyes on each other—judging each other—instead of having their eyes on God.

God's children worship, pray, celebrate communion, and interpret the Bible in different ways. After all, God designed us to be individuals. It's healthy to discuss our differences. But after all is said and done, we need to pull together as one.

Together, God's children create a picture of what God's like. We're on display for the world to see. The more closely we're unified in love, the more accurate that picture will be.

God, help me paint a clearer picture of Your love by…

Caring words, friendship, affectionate touch—
all of these have a healing quality. Why? Because we
were all created by God to give and receive love.

JACK FROST

The human contribution is the essential ingredient. It is
only in the giving of oneself to others that we truly live.

ETHEL PERCY ANDRUS

One who has been touched by grace will no longer
look on those who stray as "'those evil people" or "those
poor people who need our help." Nor must we search for
signs of "loveworthiness." Grace teaches us that God loves
because of who God is, not because of who we are.

PHILIP YANCEY

Brightness of my Father's glory,
sunshine of my Father's face,
let Your glory e'er shine on me, fill me with Your grace.

JEAN SOPHIA PIGOTT

The Time Is Ripe

[Jesus] said to them, "Come with me by yourselves
to a quiet place and get some rest."

MARK 6:31

In the century before Jesus was born, the Latin poet Horace wrote two little words that remain a popular catchphrase even today: Carpe Diem. In light of the brevity of life and our desire to use well the time God's given us, seizing the day seems like wise advice. It encourages us to burst onto the dawn of each new day fully caffeinated, motivated, and ready to go-go-go!

But the original translation of Horace's advice really means "pluck the fruit when ripe." In other words, do the right thing at the right time. Sometimes, the right thing to do is nothing at all. Believe it or not, that advice comes straight from the Bible.

After completing creation, God took a day off. He sat back and celebrated everything He'd accomplished in the last six days. He encourages you to follow His example. Life isn't all about doing. It's also about "being," simply enjoying God's good gifts and the results of your hard work. Taking a time-out isn't wasted time. It's time that's ripe for rest and renewal.

God, teach me how to "be" by letting go of...

We need quiet time to examine our lives openly
and honestly.... Spending quiet time alone gives your
mind an opportunity to renew itself and create order.

SUSAN L. TAYLOR

The faster we move the less we become;
our very speed diminishes us.

EUGENE PETERSON

Let us use texts of Scripture as fuel for our heart's fire…;
let us attend sermons, but above all,
let us be much alone with Jesus.

CHARLES H. SPURGEON

God not only orders our steps, He orders our stops.

GEORGE MUELLER

Come As You Are

Whatever you do or say, do it as a representative of the Lord Jesus, giving thanks through him to God the Father.

COLOSSIANS 3:17 NLT

If you're a woman who believes in God, it's tempting to act like the perfect child. After all, you want to put God in a positive light. If others could see all of your mistakes, your questions, and your imperfections, well…they might think God isn't that powerful after all. Right?

Wrong. Every woman who's honest with herself knows she's a work in progress. There's always room for growth. Just take a look at the heroes of the Bible, men and women alike. Often, they blew it. Sometimes, they blew it big time. We read about their failures, as well as victories, because God values authenticity and honesty.

Being open to acknowledge your struggles and doubts, as well as your successes and breakthroughs, is a real-life visual aid. It demonstrates to others that God's acceptance isn't dependent on how good we are. It's a reflection of how good He is.

Don't be afraid to be yourself. God's power can shine brightest through the true you.

God, please help me be more "real" about…

Bring your soul to the Great Physician—
exactly as you are, even and especially at your worst
moment.... For it is in such moments that you
will most readily sense His healing presence.

TERESA OF AVILA

We cannot do everything, and there is a sense
of liberation in realizing that. This enables us to do
something, and to do it very well. It may be incomplete,
but it is a beginning, a step along the way, an opportunity
for the Lord's grace to enter and do the rest. We may
never see the end results, but that is the difference
between the master builder and the worker. We are
workers, not master builders; ministers, not messiahs.
We are prophets of a future not our own.

OSCAR ROMERO

One Step at a Time

*I am the L*ORD *your God who takes hold of your right hand and says to you, Do not fear; I will help you.*

ISAIAH 41:13

As a kid, you learned how to run. You put one foot in front of the other. Pretty simple, right? But what if you wanted to run a marathon? Running that kind of race takes more than just picking up your feet while wearing expensive sneakers. It takes training and perseverance.

Not all marathons are athletic events. Some are financial. Others are relational. They can also be emotional, physical, or spiritual. Sometimes they're races you choose to run, like losing ten pounds, earning your master's degree, or raising a child. Others you may be thrown into without warning, like being diagnosed with cancer or losing your job. For the latter, there's no time to train. You may feel as though you didn't even have the chance to grab your shoes.

God's presence provides the power you need to persevere. He isn't an "easy button" that whisks you to the finish line. He's a coach, running beside you, offering perspective, strength, and encouragement every step of the way.

God, please help me keep moving forward with…

Grasp the fact that God is for you—let this certainty
make its impact on you in relation to what you are up
against at this very moment; and you will find in thus
knowing God as your sovereign protector, irrevocably
committed to you in the covenant of grace, both freedom
from fear and new strength for the fight.

J. I. PACKER

The duties God requires of us are not in proportion
to the strength we possess in ourselves. Rather,
they are proportional to the resources available
to us in Christ. We do not have the ability
in ourselves to accomplish the least of God's tasks.
This is a law of grace. When we recognize
it is impossible to perform a duty in our own strength,
we will discover the secret of its accomplishment.

JOHN OWEN

On the inside, where God is making new life, not a day goes by without his unfolding grace.

2 CORINTHIANS 4:16 MSG

Expect the Unexpected

This is the day the Lord has made;
we will rejoice and be glad in it.

PSALM 118:24 NKJV

Today may be disguised as an ordinary day. You follow the same routine. You scrub the same dishes, clothes, and face you've scrubbed before. You perform the same tasks, pass the same people, and watch the same TV shows you always do. And when you fall asleep tonight in the same bed, you think you know what tomorrow holds. But you'd be wrong.

There are no ordinary days—or ordinary people. That's because with God, anything and everything is possible. God's power and creativity are beyond what you can imagine, beyond what you would ever dare to dream. Don't limit today by what happened yesterday. The next twenty-four hours are a limited, one-time opportunity.

So wake up every morning with your eyes wide open to the potential of the day. Old habits may be broken. Relationships may be restored. Conflict may be resolved. New friends may be made. The same God who is at work in the world is at work in you. That should be enough to get you out of bed and ready for adventure.

God, my prayer for today is…

In the process of creation and relationship,
what seems mundane and trivial may show itself
to be holy, precious, part of a pattern.

LUCI SHAW

It is not objective proof of God's existence that
we want, but the experience of God's presence.
That is the miracle we are really after, and that is also,
I think, the miracle that we really get.

FREDERICK BUECHNER

If God is here for us and not elsewhere, then in fact
this place is holy and this moment is sacred.

ISABEL ANDERS

Let your religion be less of a theory
and more of a love affair.

G. K. CHESTERTON

Rooted in Faith

I am like an olive tree growing in God's Temple.
I trust God's love.

PSALM 52:8 NCV

Growth isn't always visible to the eye. It often works undercover, splitting open seeds, pushing fresh, green shoots upward toward the surface, digging sturdy roots deeper into the darkness of fertile soil.

The same is true with spiritual growth. At times you may feel you're growing by leaps and bounds. You're learning so much about who God is and seeing your life change as a result. But every growing season has its winter. There will also be times when you may feel stuck, as though no matter how much you work, pray, or read God's Word, old habits refuse to die. The warmth of God's love may feel as though it's a thing of the past. Consequently, your desire to persevere may feel like it's withering away.

When winter comes, cling to what you know about God. Trust in His unfailing love and His Spirit's power to encourage your growth. Spring will come. It's only a matter of time. Until then, don't give up drawing closer to God. Allow your roots to grow deep.

Lord, in this season of faith, help me to…

We do not understand the intricate pattern of the stars in their courses, but we know that He who created them does, and that just as surely as He guides them, He is charting a safe course for us.

BILLY GRAHAM

Acceptance says, "True, this is my situation at the moment. I'll look unblinkingly at the reality of it. But I'll also open my hands to accept willingly whatever a loving Father sends me."

CATHERINE MARSHALL

Out of your relationship with God come life's greatest treasures—fellowship, wisdom, peacefulness of soul, eternal hope, gladness of heart, direction and meaning, and a glorious purpose in all you do.

ROY LESSIN

The Secret of Success

Follow Me, and I will make you fishers of men.

MATTHEW 4:19 NKJV

Jesus's disciples understood "net worth." After all, most of them were fisherman. What they brought up in their nets was a measure of how successful their day had been. But Jesus asked His disciples to put down their nets and fish for people instead. To do this type of fishing, the disciples cast out a net of love, sharing and showing others how much God cared for them.

In God's eyes, the disciples lived successful lives. They weren't rich. They weren't well educated. They didn't have fancy titles that followed their names. Most didn't even marry or raise a family. What they did was what God asked. They devoted their lives to loving others well.

God asks you to do the very same thing. You don't have to move to some remote part of the globe to share God's love. You can follow God right where you are. Ask Him to show you the secret to leading a successful life by learning to love the same way Jesus's disciples did. Then go fish.

God, I want to be successful; teach me to...

God wants to paint a beautiful portrait
of His Son in and through your life.
A painting like no other in all of time.

JONI EARECKSON TADA

We are here such a short time. You and I will stand
in that great cloud of witnesses in the blink of an eye.
We want to be among the generations of whom Jesus
can say, "I got to do great and mighty things in that era
right there. Those people had some kind of fiery faith."
Oh, make it so, Lord Jesus. Let it be. Revive us again.

BETH MOORE

God has called us into the joyous ministry
of giving His love away to others.

DON LESSIN

Childlike Faith

Incline your ear and hear the words of the wise,
and apply your heart to my knowledge.

PROVERBS 22:17 NKJV

In the classic TV show *Dragnet* Sgt. Joe Friday is best remembered for his line, "The facts, ma'am, just the facts." In the information age in which we live, we have access to facts regarding just about anything. All we have to do is log on to the Internet.

Being knowledgeable is more than just knowing the facts. It's understanding why they matter and how they fit into the context of how we live and what we believe. So, why would Jesus tell us to have the faith of a child? Children aren't known for their expansive knowledge. True, kids don't know it all. But neither do adults. What makes children's faith so exemplary is they're aware they don't know it all. They trust those around them to teach them. They lean on others for help. They're always ready to learn, so their knowledge is growing every day.

Come to God like a child, inquisitive, trusting, and ready to learn. He'll help you apply what you know in ways that will help you grow. And that's a fact.

God, I trust You to teach me what I don't know, specifically…

Whether sixty or sixteen, there is in every
human being's heart the love of wonder, the sweet
amazement at the stars and starlike things,
the undaunted challenge of events, the unfailing
childlike appetite for what-next, and the joy of...living.

SAMUEL ULLMAN

Faith isn't the ability to believe long and far
into the misty future. It's simply taking God
at His word and taking the next step.

JONI EARECKSON TADA

Today I give it all to Jesus: my precious children,
my mate, my hopes, my plans and dreams
and schemes, my fears and failures—all. Peace
and contentment come when the struggle ceases.

GLORIA GAITHER

You're Cordially Invited

The world cannot accept [the Spirit of truth],
because it neither sees him nor knows him.
But you know him, for he lives with you and will be in you.

JOHN 14:17

Your heart beats about seventy times every minute. Every hour, your lungs take in over seven hundred breaths. You blink your eyes more than twenty thousand times each day. But God's gift of life is more than heartbeats and respiration. It's things like joy, love, growth, and purpose.

When God set your heart beating in your mother's womb, He did more than turn a switch to the on position. He extended an invitation to join Him in celebrating an unparalleled adventure. But to join the celebration, you need to do more than receive an invitation. You also need to accept it.

It may take awhile to understand God's invitation, to believe He's at work behind the scenes. It may take even longer to accept it, to reach out in humility and say, "I believe." But once you do, that's when your life truly begins.

One day, your heart will stop beating. But this new life will continue. Your adventure with God is one that never ends.

Lord, accepting Your invitation means that I…

Where are you? Start there. Openly and freely declare
your need to the One who cares deeply.

CHARLES R. SWINDOLL

Lift up your eyes. Your heavenly Father waits
to bless you—in inconceivable ways to make your
life what you never dreamed it could be.

ANNE ORTLUND

Even though God may be unknown to us, He is near
and willing to reveal Himself. God has promised that
"if you look for me wholeheartedly, you will find me"
(Jeremiah 29:13 [NLT]). Turning over our will involves
accepting God as He is instead of insisting on creating
Him in our own image. When we seek God with
an open heart and mind, we will find Him.

STEPHEN ARTERBURN

A Legacy of Love

The world and its desires pass away,
but whoever does the will of God lives forever.

1 JOHN 2:17

You're walking through this life on the sands of time. Each step you take leaves a footprint, marking a path for those who come after you. One day those footprints will stop in their tracks, and you'll begin walking on a heavenly shore. At that moment, you'll leave behind property, possessions, and perhaps a few items on your bucket list. But those footprints will remain, a legacy of how you've lived your life. Will they leave a path worth following?

You can work hard to make a name for yourself, to accumulate things of value so you can leave a substantial inheritance behind. But in the long run, the legacy of your love has the power to outlast and outshine them all. Keep in mind that what you choose to do today is what forms those indelible footsteps. Your words, your generosity, your attentiveness, your compassion, your faith… if those you love followed your lead, would you rejoice at where your footsteps led them?

Plan for the future. Live a life of love today.

God, the kind of legacy I want to leave is…